SERIES EDITOR

Dr. Sally Monsour

Professor of Music Education
Georgia State University
Atlanta

Music in Early Childhood

by Dr. John M. Batcheller

Professor of Music Education
University of New Mexico
Albuquerque

Classroom Music Enrichment Units

THE CENTER FOR APPLIED RESEARCH IN EDUCATION, INC.
521 FIFTH AVENUE, NEW YORK, N.Y. 10017

Cover photograph by Allen Madans,
Albuquerque, N.M.

Library of Congress Cataloging in Publication Data

Batcheller, John.
  Music in early childhood.

  (Classroom music enrichment units)
  Bibliography: p.
  1. School music--Instruction and study--United
States. 2. Music--Instruction and study--Juvenile.
I. Title. II. Series.
MT3.U5B33   372.8'7'044   74-31204
ISBN 0-87628-212-5

Printed in the United States of America

About This Handbook

This handbook was written to meet the continuing demand for classroom teachers who can guide the musical activities of young children. It provides many simple, tested music experiences with all of the details and directions you will need to use them, today, with your own pupils. Hopefully, these activities will help you come closer to realizing the ideal of "music for every child."

Each of the ideas in the handbook takes into consideration that music is purposeful and that children should use it like language and dramatic play—to add vividness and meaning to the acts of growing, living, and learning. With this in mind, you should try to create an environment that is not bound by rigid formalities of certain prescribed methods employed in formal, set-apart periods. Rather, you are encouraged to try these ideas whenever and wherever emotion and imagination on the child's part are ready to respond. Music then becomes an integral part of the child's daily school life. Whether it is teaching concepts of high-low; left-right; forward-backward; vowel awareness; squares, circles, and triangles; word recognition or counting, music enriches each activity.

Also, as you become more at ease in directing the experiences presented here, you will discover and begin to feel the close relationship that exists between a child's inner needs and his expressive behavior. In this respect, singing and moving are perhaps the most personal and intimate. There are so many learning experiences that are projected through song participation and rhythmic movement. For this reason, the handbook contains many lesson ideas using vocal play, chanting, and rhythmic movements.

Children in their early years need experiences that build up and strengthen their self-image. The musical experiences in this handbook are especially suited to encourage individual recognition as well as group awareness. They should therefore help avoid the antagonism and indifference that often result from dividing children into groups such as "bluebirds and blackbirds," producers and consumers, performers and listeners, singers and nonsingers, gifted and nongifted.

"Getting going" in the beginning years of a child's life is more important than "getting ready." And direct involvement is the best way to "get going." For this reason, all of the music experiences in the handbook embody participation.

Children in early childhood are born "makers" and "doers," or, put another way, "participators." Very young boys and girls learn to talk by talking and, in like manner, they learn music by making music. Hopefully, the ideas given here will assist you so that your children can be expressive in many musically "active" ways—all leading toward the end of musical involvement and sensitivity.

John M. Batcheller

Contents

About This Handbook 3

1 Rhythm and Movement 7

Feeling the Beat—7
   Freddie the Frog—7
   Bear Steps—9
   Making and Using Poi Balls—9

Rhythm in Words—11
   Scraping Rhythm—12
   "Moving" Words—12

Movement Improvisation and Expression—13
   Follow-the-Leader Game—13
   Movement with Colored Fabrics—13
   Rhythm with Scissors—14
   Moving to Floating Objects—14

2 Singing 16

Discovering the Singing Voice—16
   Singing vs. Speaking—16
   Vocal Involvement—18

Early Singing Skills—18
   Voice Ranges—19
   Tone Matching—19
   Remedial Ideas—20
   Getting Started—21

Self-Expression Through Singing—22
   Song Improvisations—22

3 Basic Skills Through Music 24

Directional Concepts—25
   Visual Fugue Activity—25
   Moving with Parachute Silk—26

Movement on a Pair of Stairs—28

Tactile Awareness Through Texture—28
Making and Using a Texture Box—28

Number Recognition and Counting—30
Musical Numbers—31
Counting and Listening—31

Building Language Awareness—33
Vowels and Consonants—33
Eye Span—35

Shape Recognition—36
Elastic Ropes—37

Developing a Positive Self-Image—41
Encouraging Personal Response—41
Stimulating Individualism—42

4 Music Interest Centers   44

Starting a Classroom Music Center—44
Using the Interest Center—45
The Music Store—46

Manipulative Objects—48
Communications Column—48
Miniature Keyboards—49
Sound Makers—50

Games—51
Fish Pond—51

5 Individualized Music Lessons   53

Guidelines for Making a Tape—53
Lesson: Concepts of Fast and Slow—54
Lesson: Concepts of Upward-Downward; Steps-Skips—55

Usefulness Resources   60

Teacher References—60
Song and Game Books—62
Recordings for Singing and Moving—62
Basic Series Publications—64

1

Rhythm and Movement

To say that children like to become personally involved in a musical experience is an understatement. Young children and music "go together." They need to have opportunities with music that allow them to "let go" and express their physical and emotional natures.

This involvement is best demonstrated by bodily responses to the element of rhythm. Rhythms and childhood go together in a direct and very meaningful way. Children are always moving and responding to repeated forms of rhythmic beats as in rope jumping, playing jacks, or just jumping up and down with glee at a humorous or exciting event. In fact, this is such an obvious point when dealing with early childhood education, that teachers need hardly be reminded that rhythmic games, dances, movement experiences, and vocal rhythm chanting are an important aspect of a well-balanced program of development.

FEELING THE BEAT

In early childhood an important feeling to develop has to do with the very life within the music—the steady beat. The following three activities are designed both to give children opportunities to "become" the beat and feel this phenomenon actually happen to them in a physical sense.

Freddie the Frog

Try making a cloth beanbag in the shape of a frog (see the pattern in Figure 1-1). Fill the bag with two pounds of small dried beans or lentils. The frog shape should be made of strong material and sewn with heavy thread because it will take a beating.

Next, teach the children the following limerick using a spoken heavy accent where indicated.

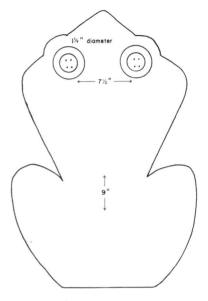

Cut two forms using this pattern. A piece of heavy green upholstery cloth would be excellent. Place the forms together and sew around the edge with nylon thread leaving about a one-inch opening. Turn the form inside out through the opening and fill with beans or lentils. Close the inch opening. Use buttons for the eyes and let your imagination go for any further decoration.

Figure 1-1   Pattern for Freddie the Frog

Freddie the Frog

Freddie the frog, sat on a log
Looking for something to eat. . . .
A big juicy fly is a sight for his eye,
And for Freddie would be quite a treat.

After they have learned the limerick, ask six of the children to form a circle with the children standing about four feet apart.

Using the beanbag frog, have one child begin to toss the frog on the accented beats to the child next to him in a clockwise direction. The child who ends up with the frog when the limerick is finished is out of the circle, and the game continues until there is one child left who can be said to have "won."

When the children become truly aware of what the game is about, they can then begin to toss the bag to anyone in the circle instead of clockwise. This adds more excitement and offers an element of surprise. Finally, when they have become agile at this and can make passes on the accented words of the limerick, play a recording of a slow, steady piece of music and invite children to toss the frog to each other on the music's heavy accents or beats. The transition from the accented words of the limerick to the accented beats in the music is generally quite successful.

NOTE: When the children begin to toss the frog to the beat of the music, it is a good idea to play the recording quite loud for its obvious stimulation. (A suggested selection is RCA Adventures in Listening, Grade 1, Berlioz, *Damnation of Faust.*)

This activity allows children to truly "feel" the beats as they toss and receive the frog. It also assists them in achieving better muscular coordination—always a major concern with children of this age.

Bear Steps

The next activity involves using "The Bear Went Over the Mountain" with these words:

1. Hammer away with one hammer,
   Hammer away with one hammer,
   Hammer away with one hammer,
   Just hammer and hammer all day.
2. Hammer away with two hammers (etc.)
3. Hammer away with three hammers (etc.)
4. Hammer away with four hammers (etc.)

Children should sit on the floor for this activity with their legs straight out in front of them and hands made into fists on the floor at each side. They can sit in any formation they desire as long as they are out of each other's way. While everyone sings, the children pound the floor with one fist throughout the first verse. Encourage them to keep their pounding in time with the song.

During the singing of the second verse, the children pound on the floor with both fists to represent the two hammers in the song. With the third verse, they pound one heel along with their two fists, and on the fourth verse, add the other heel so each child will be pounding with his own four "hammers."

Because of the total physical involvement in this activity, it is easy to see that the children soon come to grasp the concept of keeping steady accented beats.

Making and Using Poi Balls

Another activity that helps children become more conscious of underlying steady beats is the use of Poi Balls, which are found throughout Polynesia. The natives there use them in connection with folk singing and dancing.

Making Poi Balls

Poi Balls can be easily made by the children with some guidance from you. Here are directions:

1. Cut three strands of heavy knitting yarn in lengths about three feet long and braid them together. Different-colored yarns lend a more interesting effect.
2. Knot one end of the braided yarn and slip it through a small cardboard disc with a hole punched in it (see Figure 1-2).
3. Make small wads out of paper towels. Pack the paper wads around the disc and bind them together with strips of masking tape to form the shape of a ball. Imbedding the cardboard disc within the paper wads prevents the knotted yarn from pulling out of the finished ball.
4. Continue to bind wads of paper towels around the yarn with the masking tape until a rather solid ball is formed, about the size of a tennis ball.
5. Wrap the finished ball very tightly with a piece of plastic. (A plastic refrigerator bag or dry cleaning garment bag works nicely.) Tie the plastic around the braided yarn with a strong piece of string and trim off excess plastic neatly.
6. Knot or tie off the other end of the braided yarn.

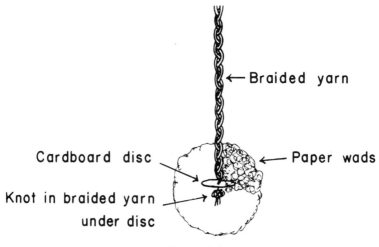

Braided yarn

Cardboard disc

Paper wads

Knot in braided yarn under disc

Figure 1-2

Using the Poi Balls

To use the Poi Balls with music, give each child a pair of balls—one for each hand. Then demonstrate and direct children in the following procedure:

1. Wrap the braided yarn a few turns around each hand so the balls dangle 18 to 20 inches at each side of the child.
2. Begin to swing the balls in circles away from the body with a forward motion from the wrist.
3. Be certain to keep the arms quiet with elbows against the body at the waist. All swinging action should be generated from the wrists (see Figure 1-3).

Figure 1-3

NOTE: Once the technique is acquired, it becomes a simple matter to synchronize the swinging Poi Balls with various kinds of rhythm.

4. Start with a steady, slow, duple rhythm like "Row, Row, Row Your Boat," and gradually increase the tempo until both hands are able to manipulate the Poi Balls in time to the music.

This activity is a natural to increase awareness of beats in the music as the entire body begins to feel the rhythm and the whole idea of a steady, ongoing rhythm is picked up in the swinging balls.

RHYTHM IN WORDS

It is valuable to use the natural speech of young children in order to build a rhythmic experience. Such experiences could include everything from simple chanting of familiar words within the child's interest level, to the use of words as a point of departure for bodily movement. The following are examples.

Scraping Rhythm

Use a Guiro (Mexican scraping, percussion instrument) or an old washboard with a small stick to scrape the rhythm of various words derived from objects or pictures placed before the class. Start with only two objects selected from the classroom such as a *pencil box* and the *wastepaper basket*. Invite the children to look at both of the objects and talk about them. Then, scrape the rhythm of one of them and ask someone to tell you which one was scraped. These objects might be scraped as follows:

Pencil box ——— ——— ———
Wastepaper basket ———— ——— ——— ———— ————

Eventually, increase the objects one by one until the children are asked to identify the rhythm of one object from a group of five objects. Pictures can also be used in the same way. This activity calls attention to the rhythm of speech and increases memory span.

"Moving" Words

To acquaint young children with words that imply movement, it is helpful to give them experiences that allow them to create and become these meanings. Obvious words like "run" can be easily understood when associated with a deer or a horse. Here, a child can actually run and pretend he is a deer or a horse. However, when the word "run" is associated with water or a motor, different connotations are evoked. To accomplish this, you might ask the class to run like water or run like a motor standing in place using only their bodies. In this way, new meanings are made very real and the child becomes personally involved with the meanings.

Below are listed some suggestions to use as starters for this activity. It is always beneficial to talk about what is being done and to call attention to various children who seem to grasp the meanings of words through their movements.

- Grow like weed.
- Hop like a frog.
- Shine like a star.
- Wiggle like a snake.
- Spin like a top.
- Bloom like a flower.
- Sparkle like a diamond.
- Glide like a rocket.
- Stretch like a rubber band.
- Open like a bud.
- Wave like a flag.
- Sway like a branch.

- Rise like the sun.
- Set like the moon.
- Climb like a vine.
- Fly like a bird.

- Knot like a rope.
- Wither like a rose.
- Twist like a cable.
- Dance like a moonbeam.

MOVEMENT IMPROVISATION AND EXPRESSION

Almost every rhythmic experience has within it the element of self-expression. This in turn provides the materials through which children can make up their own movement ideas—adding new motions, changing the tempo of their movement, or suggesting new rhythmic patterns.

Follow-the-Leader Game

Here is a kind of movement call-and-response activity that is helpful in developing a feeling of ensemble, steady beats, and extemporaneous creativity.

Have all the children involved sit facing center in a circle. Lead them in chanting the following in a 4 rhythm:

PIDDLE-RIDDLE,　PIDDLE-RIDDLE　BOO!　BOO!

Still keeping the framework of this rhythm, the teacher, or any designated leader, does some manner of movement with her head, fingers, hands, arms, or torso immediately following the chant. When the leader completes her movement, the children in the circle do an exact imitation of it followed by everyone, once again, reciting the chant in rhythm. The child at the right of the leader then creates another movement in his own way, which is imitated by the group, and so on around the circle until everyone has had a turn.

Movement with Colored Fabrics

Using different-colored fabrics, designate various kinds of movement to correspond with the colors of the fabric. While a recording of some interesting mood music is playing, wave a piece of colored fabric to signal how the children are to move.

Begin this activity with only two kinds of movement and add others as children's abilities at moving and memories expand. The following are a few suggestions for movement:

Red	fast movement	Blue	slow movement
Green	uneven movement	Black	spooky movement
White	freeze in place	Brown	heavy movement
Yellow	high, stretching move-ment with long steps	Pink	low, bending move-ment with small steps

Rhythm with Scissors

Give five or six children each a pair of blunt-end (round point) scissors. Seat them in a circle and place a number of used pieces of typing paper in front of them. Next, invite them to cut strips of paper in time to the rhythm of an appropriate piece of music. A moderately slow march is excellent. After children have grasped the idea of the activity, limit their cutting time and see who finishes with the most strips of paper.

NOTE: This is a fine activity for small muscle development as well as learning to manipulate a pair of scissors.

Moving to Floating Objects

Music can be valuable to teach young children to move in slow and graceful ways. Their natural tendencies at this early age result in fast, jerky, awkward and uneven movements. To help them to recognize and feel grace in their own movement, the following two ideas using bottles often produce good results.

Find a very tall glass olive bottle or any tall narrow glass container, the taller the better for this activity. Fill the bottle with a very heavy transparent pancake or waffle syrup. Select a colorful small glass marble and place it in the bottle. Seal the bottle very tightly with its original cover so no syrup can escape when the bottle is tilted (Figure 1-4). When the marble has reached the bottom of the bottle, invert the bottle and invite the children to watch it slowly drift down through the syrup to the bottom of the bottle. Do this several times, then ask the children to stand very tall and pretend they are the marble and very slowly sink to the floor.

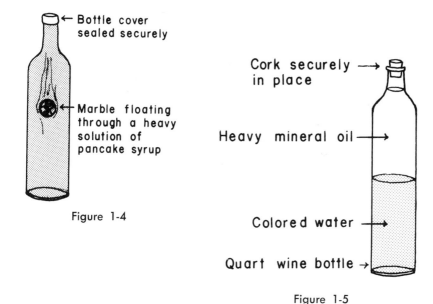

Bottle cover
sealed securely

Marble floating
through a heavy
solution of
pancake syrup

Figure 1-4

Cork securely →
in place

Heavy mineral oil →

Colored water →

Quart wine bottle →

Figure 1-5

NOTE: Appropriate music such as a lullaby should be played while this activity is in progress.

The second idea accomplishes the same thing, utilizing a larger bottle, colored water, and heavy mineral oil. For this, obtain a quart bottle and fill it half full of water colored with some vegetable dye. (A deep blue-green is good for this activity.) Then, fill the remaining space in the bottle with heavy mineral oil and cork the bottle securely (see Figure 1-5). The two liquids will separate immediately.

When the apparatus is completed, ask a child to cradle the bottle on its side in both hands and slowly tip it back and forth in a rocking movement. The liquids within will form undulating waves that resemble the ocean's surf. Perhaps some children will imagine the bottle to be a piece of the sky and the forms inside as clouds being changed by soft winds. All the children will want to take a turn rocking the bottle to create this intriguing sight.

When everyone has had his turn, invite the children to lie on the floor and close their eyes and recall in their minds the waves and clouds they created with the bottle. Then play a recording of Debussy's "La Mer" and suggest that the children become waves, wind, or clouds.

2

Singing

Joining with others in a singing experience is a rewarding and valuable part of the music program in early childhood. A large variety of songs about every phase of a child's experience should be in the repertory of the program. These include songs of nature, country, home, family, community, game songs, and songs the child composes himself.

DISCOVERING THE SINGING VOICE

In human development, the act of speech follows the act of singing. Children communicate by "singing" long before they are able physically or intellectually to form actual speech patterns. As helpless infants, they vocalize their needs in songlike fashion and their repertories are quite extensive. There are "arias" one could describe as the "Hungry" aria, the "Wet" aria, "There's-a-Pin-Sticking-in-Me" aria, "Pick Me Up" aria, "I'm Cold" aria, "I Need Some Loving" aria, and many variations of the "I Am Happy and Contented" aria. Generally, the child's physical or emotional condition is hopefully improved once he has rendered his "aria." For this reason, the act of "singing" is a strong, positive expression at the beginning of a child's life.

Singing vs. Speaking

The first thing you should establish with boys and girls is that they have two kinds of voices—a speaking voice and a singing voice. One way of bringing this to their attention is to tell them a story using your speaking voice. Emphasize this point throughout the demonstration. Try reciting a story such as the following:

> I know a cat who says "Me-ow,"
> I know a dog who says "Bow-wow,"
> Every time I bring them chow.
> Early in the morning.

After children have heard the story, ask them to say the words "me-ow" and "bow-wow," using their speaking voices, when they appear in the story. Repeat the story and direct them to join in. Next, tell the children you are going to tell the story again using your other voice called a "singing" voice. The song in Figure 2-1

Figure 2-1

is an illustration of one that fits with the story. Finally, ask the children to use their "singing" voices to join in on "me-ow" and "bow-wow" as you repeat the song again.

After children have discovered the difference between their speaking and singing voices, they can begin to use them correctly and easily. One of the first and most important things to practice is to take in enough air to keep their singing voices going. To accomplish this, ask the children to take a deep breath and see who can hold it the longest. Next, have them take another deep breath and make a singing sound on "Ah" or "Oo" or "Oh." Again, see who can hold it for the longest time. Also, ask them to see how much of a familiar song they can sing on one breath. "Are You Sleeping" is a good song for this.

NOTE: These breathing experiences should become part of each day's routine.

To further establish the differences between the speaking voice and the singing voice, ask children to respond to the following immediately after this kind of experience:

1. Which voice do you like best? Why?
2. Can you describe your singing voice?
3. What makes your singing voice different from your speaking voice?

4. Mary, ask Veronica a question using your speaking voice.
5. Tina, ask Steve a question using your singing voice.
6. Let's use our singing voice for three minutes as we discuss what we are going to do today.

Vocal Involvement

Another way to help children discover their singing voices is to have them respond vocally to being objects that bring out a song feeling such as suggested in the short songs in Figure 2-2.

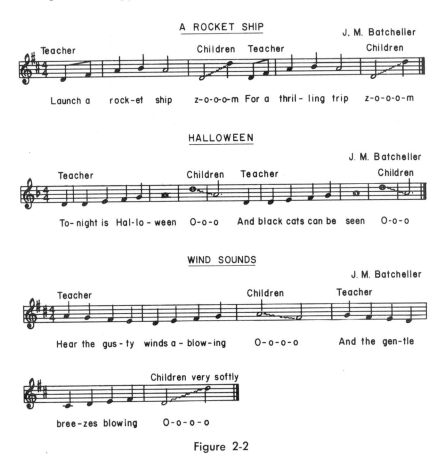

Figure 2-2

EARLY SINGING SKILLS

You do not have to "sell" a child on the idea of singing. He already loves to sing and, for the most part, enjoys singing. Singing, however, is a skill and as a skill can be improved in many ways. These ways are certainly the responsibility of early childhood education.

Voice Ranges

The voice range of young children is usually limited. In fact, many professional music educators agree that the natural "call" of childhood should be the point of departure for early singing experiences. This "call" is made up of a descending interval of three tones, as in sol-me, or 5-3 of a major scale. It is also referred to as a falling minor third. As the child's voice develops, the range increases so that by the age of six the best overall singing range is approximately six tones as shown on the staff in Figure 2-3. Flexibility and a wider range are developed very quickly when adequate singing experiences are provided. By the time the children are eight years old, most songs can be pitched within the limits of the treble clef supplemented by two lower neighbors (see Figure 2-4).

Figure 2-3   Vocal Range of Six-year-olds

Figure 2-4   Vocal Range of Eight-year-olds

Tone Matching

Undoubtedly, the problems relating to pitch are among the most common when working with young children. Children with pitch problems can be described as follows:

- children who cannot match a given pitch;
- children who cannot carry a tune with the rest of the class;
- children who cannot discern whether a pitch goes up or down.

In order to correct these problems and bring about an awareness of pitch, many musical experiences should be given to children each day. Tone matching is an excellent way to start. Here, you can begin by calling the roll on a falling minor third interval. The children can respond by singing back on the same pitches, "Present" or "Here I am" or whatever response seems fitting. During this time, you can hear which children have a pitch problem.

> NOTE: It is strongly cautioned that at no time should a child be made to feel threatened or embarrassed.

Helpful replies to children's responses might be:

- "Good for Alice! She did it today."
- "That's better Carl."
- "Listen carefully before you answer so you can hear the pitches."
- "Just a little higher (or lower) Bill, and I believe you have it."
- "Let's everyone call Betty's name."

Tone matching games using the names of fruit, animals, vegetables, or room objects can be played. It is a good idea for the children to match each other's voices instead of only your voice—once they understand what it is all about. Once you discover which children are in any pitch difficulty, you can begin to use remedial work. Again, the obvious failures should never be singled out.

Remedial Ideas

Following are a variety of techniques for helping children who have difficulties with pitch.

For the child weak in maintaining pitch:

1. Place the child in front of and between two strong (pitchwise) singers. In this way, the child weak in pitch will hear it coming at him in three directions.
2. Sing many well-liked, familiar songs to gain tonal security.
3. Play tone-matching games on the bells as well as vocally.
4. Sing with sustained vowels such as "loo" and "la" instead of using words. This will place focus on the melodic line rather than the text.
5. Select songs having a limited range of only a few pitches. ("I Know a Cat," page 16, is a good example of such a song.)

For the child who cannot detect the rise and fall in pitches:

1. Use hand levels to accompany all singing. To do this, place the hand, palm down, in front at chest level. When the melody goes up, indicate this by raising the hand; when it goes down, lower the hand. This is an excellent way to show wide and narrow intervals.
2. Use visual devices to link special concepts with pitch concepts. Going up and down stairs and climbing up and down a ladder are excellent for this. This stepwise movement of scale passages can easily be seen in this manner.

For the child who sings out of tune:

1. Use many tone-matching games.
2. Have the child pretend to be a toothpaste tube. He should be standing with feet together imagining that the cap of the tube in his head. Gently squeeze his waist with an upward pressure to push the tone (toothpaste) higher. For this, use a sustained tone.
3. For the child who sings above the given pitch, gently pull an earlobe to pretend to let some air out to lower the pitch.
4. Ask the children to extend an arm in a rigid manner to simulate a pump handle. As they sustain a tone, pump the arm to raise the pitch if they are singing below the given pitch.
5. When a child is singing an entire song along with the class, but in another key, find the key in which he is singing and have the class sing the song in his key. At this point, it is easier for the class to match the child's pitch than for the child to struggle with the change. Gradually, bring them together until the child senses that he is "in tune."
6. Quietly sing a pitch to a child and ask him to carry it to another child at the end of the room. This is also a fine way to develop a musical memory.

Getting Started

Beginning singers need a lot of security before and during the learning of new songs. Always have the children listen to either the teacher's singing or a recording of the song to be learned. After they have heard it, discuss the text. From the text, the style and type of song can be determined. Songs about frisky animals would naturally be sung with a gay lilt, and songs about bedtime and going to sleep would be sung slowly and quietly.

It is most important to establish the starting pitch of the song. You can begin directions by chanting on that pitch. Once this is done, set the cadence by chanting, "One, two, ready, sing." Children will follow your voice more than they will any form of formal conducting beat. For this reason, simply conduct them with an expressive hand movement to match the rhythmic feeling in the song. It is sometimes effective to overact "mouthing" the words in order to help the children remember the text.

SELF-EXPRESSION THROUGH SINGING

Numerous songbooks are published containing excellent song materials within the appropriate range and within the child's interest and vocabulary. (See "Song and Game Books," p. 62, for several examples.) However, there are also many creative ways to encourage expression through the use of the voice. The following activity is a good way to begin this type of expression and creative musical interpretation.

Song Improvisations

THE EARTH AND I

J. M. Batcheller

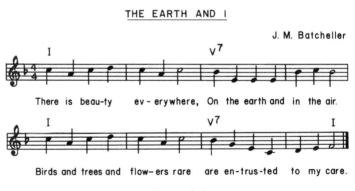

Figure 2-5

Teach the children the song in Figure 2-5 several days before you put this activity together so they will be thoroughly familiar with it. This will free them to think about other things while they are singing.

When young children sing, they frequently produce a careless rendition and attempt to beat each other to the end of the song. This is easily remedied with some attention paid to how songs are to be sung. To help youngsters in developing some style and expression in their singing, ask them to sing the song they have learned in different ways reflecting "who" or "what" might be doing the singing. In this way they will be drawn into singing from different vantage points. Each of these points would obviously produce a different rendition.

Here are some ideas to help you guide children in this activity:

1. Sing the song like a giant would sing it.
2. Sing the song like a small white mouse would sing it.
3. Sing the song like a mean old cat would sing it.
4. Sing the song like a lazy mule would sing it.
5. Sing the song like a swift road runner would sing it.
6. Sing the song like a mechanical doll winding down would sing it.

NOTE: After each rendition, it is helpful to discuss the difference in each way the song was sung.

Exploring Sounds and Learning to Share

3

Basic Skills Through Music

As a teacher of young children, you are naturally concerned with very early developmental skills. These include physical, mental, and emotional abilities of every description.

Let's begin with directional concepts. In the majority of cases, try to use whole-body movements to "experience" directions of left-right, forward-backward, and up-down. Also, use objects in the home, familiar places and scenes, and everyday childhood events to capture the attention of the child, which will then focus on the direction skill and, hopefully, the concepts of relative directions that you are striving for.

Tactile sensory experiences can also help children perceive differences in word descriptions such as rough, smooth, hard, soft, and so on. These lead to the building of language awareness and vocabulary, which become permanently impressed upon the memory because they were actually "performed," so to speak.

Other skills that you can help young children develop through music have to do with number recognition and even counting. Rhythmic speech responses are directly related to "felt" repetitions of numbers and children enjoy such experiences as gamelike when they involve motion and physical energy.

Finally, it will be a joyous occasion when you observe a child's self-image grow through the confidence that comes from participation in a music program. Each child can have a creative idea that you can then incorporate into lessons on individuality, conduct, gesture, and personal relationships.

DIRECTIONAL CONCEPTS

The following three activities reinforce the directional concepts of left-right, forward-backward, and up-down through participation in musical experiences. To bring these words and their meanings into the child's awareness, it is suggested that throughout the movement experience you continually verbalize the words "left," "right," "forward," "backward," "up" and "down."

Visual Fugue Activity

The first activity might be thought of as "Visualizing a Fugue." Very young children will think of it as a game, but children in the upper grades could find it very meaningful when they are exploring the fugue through their listening activities. To insure success with younger children, they must know how to sing "Three Blind Mice." Once they are comfortable with the words and melody, select sixteen children who will form a square using four children on each side.

Rehearse each side on the movements that accompany the song (see below). Each of the four children representing a side will move as a group throughout the activity.

Song Words	*Movement Directions*
"Three blind mice"	Three steps <u>forward</u> *

---

* Underscored directional words for teacher's vocal emphasis.

"Three blind mice" .... Three steps <u>backward</u>

"See how they run" .... Three steps <u>backward</u>

"See how they run" .... Three steps <u>forward</u>

"They all run after the
farmer's wife" .... Turn <u>right</u> and take three
steps <u>forward</u>

"She cuts off their tails
with a carving knife .... Remain facing <u>right</u> and
take three steps <u>backward</u>

"Did you ever see such a
sight in your life" .... Turn <u>left</u> and take three
steps <u>backward</u>

"As three blind mice" .... Three steps <u>forward</u>

When the four children on each side of the square know these basic movements, it is time to put it all together. Side 1 begins singing and moving the complete song, repeating it four times. Side 2 begins to sing and move the song when Side 1 reaches these words, "See how they run," exactly as they would in singing a round. Side 2 continues singing the song four times. Sides 3 and 4 enter in like manner. When each side finishes singing and moving, they remain standing in place until the last side (4) finishes.

This activity not only helps to create an awareness of direction, but also gives children the opportunity to experience the element of harmony. It is also fun both to participate in and to observe. From this experience boys and girls can quickly come to know those directional commands indicating right and left, forward and backward. At the same time they are acquiring vocal independence by singing the round while actually moving.

Moving with Parachute Silk

Another activity to reinforce the concepts of left-right and forward-backward uses thin, light fabric. Large pieces of fabric materials are an invaluable part of the equipment for all early childhood music classes. A good source of such materials is a surplus store where army parachutes may be purchased inexpensively. Assuming that one of these parachutes can be found, trim off all ropes and heavy stitching and cut up the parachute in large eighty-inch squares. (Several of these can be cut from one chute.)

If a parachute cannot be purchased, use double-size nylon bed-sheets. Some cold-water dye might be used to add to the visual aspect of the activity.

When the squares have been trimmed, cut, and dyed, they are ready to be used by children. Have one child hold each corner of the square of material. Depending on the age and size of the children, another child could hold the material midway between each corner.

From here on, the possibilities are limitless. The activity might begin by allowing the children to explore several ways of manipulating the material—bending over it near the floor, holding it waist high, and stretching it way up over their heads. At any of these levels they can hold it tightly and make little shallow quivering hand motions to create ripples across the material or by holding it loosely and moving it slowly up and down, creating a condition like rolling waves. Once these possibilities are discovered, the children can begin to move to the *left* and to the *right*. Then, all facing the center of the cloth, they can walk *forward* as they raise the material over their heads, causing a billowing umbrella that can be brought back to its original position by the children walking slowly *backward*.

As soon as all of these interesting ways of treating the material are experienced, play recordings of different styles of music and allow the children to manipulate the fabric in ways they feel are suggested by the music. The following list of musical suggestions will assist you in collecting recordings to be used with this activity.

- Soft, flowing music
- Music with irregular accents
- Music with regular, heavy accents
- Music depicting scenes and events
- Abstract music
- Very slow music
- Very fast music

It is important that you point out the relationship of the type of music the children are hearing with the kinds of movements they create. In this way, that can perceive and recognize what is actually going on in the music. It can be seen that during the exploration stage of this activity when you are verbalizing the directions, the children are becoming increasingly aware of the meaning of those directional words.

NOTE: Several groups of children can participate in this activity in an outdoor setting. This adds greatly to the esthetic nature of the movements.

Movement on a Pair of Stairs

An excellent addition to the learning materials inventory in all early childhood classrooms is a four-step pair of stairs with a railing attached both up and down. These should be thirty inches wide with six-inch treads and risers. A carpenter will build one of these for a reasonable fee.

Using this stair prop, have each child go up and down to an easy 4 rhythm. Insist the children walk up and down tread by tread alternating left foot with right foot on each beat. Setting this activity to music pulls the children along and helps them gain poise and body balance as they learn to manipulate walking up and down stairs correctly. This prop is also a good aid for distinguishing melodies that move by steps and skips.

TACTILE AWARENESS THROUGH TEXTURE

Children can relate concepts of feeling through the senses of touch and hearing. The child's fingers "tell" him that whatever he is touching feels smooth, rough, sharp, thick, jagged, wet, sandy, lumpy, or oily. Likewise, his ears can "tell" him about the texture or feel of a melody, a rhythmic pattern, or the harmonic treatment in music. However, the latter is abstract and frequently children are at a loss for words to describe such feelings.

Making and Using a Texture Box

An interesting way to introduce children to musical textures is through use of a "texture box."

Construction directions

To make a texture box, first obtain a sturdy cardboard show box or any other cardboard box of that particular shape. Make certain that the box has a strong cover, because it is important that children not see what is inside. Carefully cut out an oval opening

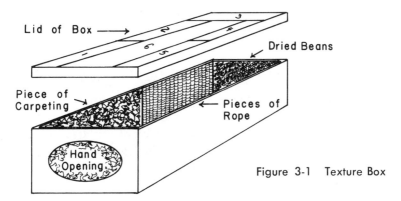

Figure 3-1   Texture Box

from one of the short sides of the box large enough to accommodate a child's hand (see Figure 3-1).

Next, look around the classroom or outside for various items that have different textural qualities. Some suggestions are: dried beans, rice, elbow macaroni, sandpaper, cotton, pieces of carpet, a square plastic sponge, small pebbles, dirt, gravel, pieces of cloth, twigs, and a piece of smooth glass. The possibilities are limitless.

When various items have been collected, remove the lid from the box and consider the three sides of the box itself. One side is opposite the opening cut for the child's hand; the other two sides are at the right and left of this opening (see Figure 3-1). Line these three sides and the floor of the box with some of the items you have assembled.

> NOTE: It is best to select no more than six items to represent various kinds of textures, from the very rough to the very smooth. Too many textures could confuse the children.

To affix the items selected, simply apply a thick coating of glue on the sides and floor of the box, attach the textural items, and allow the glue to thoroughly harden. For example, you could glue a piece of thick carpeting to one side of the box and pieces of rope on the other half. On the side opposite the hand opening, dried beans could be attached. On the floor of the box might be glued a small beveled mirror. (When using glass, choose only beveled glass because sharp edges could cut the children's fingers.) The remaining side could be divided between strips of cotton and pieces of sandpaper.

Clearly mark the cover of the texture box with numbers from

one to six showing places on the sides and floor of the box where different kinds of textures might be explored. Now the box is ready to use.

Using the texture box

Place the cover on the box and secure it with a large rubber band. Invite one child to put his hand through the oval opening and, with his fingers, gently feel the surface of the area marked 1. As suggested previously, this area might have a piece of thick carpeting attached to it. Then ask the child to feel the side marked 3, which, in this case, has dried beans glued to it. Next, ask the child to verbalize what he feels. Words such as "soft" and "squashy" in contrast to words like "bumpy" and "hard" might be expected. However, whatever the child comes up with is acceptable as long as he feels a difference and names it. Now play a selected recording that has a smooth, even melodic line such as Foster's "Beautiful Dreamer" or Mancini's version of "If." Ask the child which textures, 1 or 3, he feels match or fit the sound of the music he is hearing. Play the recording for only thirty seconds and then stop and allow the child to explore 1 and 3 again before he makes his choice.

> NOTE: After the child has chosen, ask him to explain the reasons for his choice. Verbalizing is important since it is hoped that children will be able to express their feelings in relation to what they hear in the music.

There is no limit to the ways this texture box can be used. Attention can be directed to one musical element alone, such as rhythm, or even harmony. For the very young, the general, overall impact of whatever they hear is enough to get them started toward a directed listening experience. The reverse is also excellent—asking the child to choose a texture and then, given three choices, select the one recording he feels is a match. It is great fun in a class to prepare five or six of these texture boxes with the same numbered texture areas so several children can participate at the same time. This activity can also take place at a learning center with recorded instructions put on a cassette.

NUMBER RECOGNITION AND COUNTING

Very young children should be given many opportunities to

become familiar with numbers and to recognize them in proper sequence. By combining these learnings with a gamelike activity set to music, boys and girls can explore our numbering system in an enjoyable manner.

Musical Numbers

To play Musical Numbers, all that is needed is a set of numbers from 1 through 10 individually printed on 8″ x 10″ pieces of cardboard. These can easily be made by the teacher or purchased from a school supply house.

Next, you should become at ease with singing the number recognition song, "Numbers in a Line," (Figure 3-2), with either guitar or autoharp accompaniment.

Each verse in the song concerns itself with a different number, beginning with a definite statement about that particular number, e.g., "This is a one, it looks like a one," etc. At this point in the song, give one of the children the card with a "1" on it and ask the child to hold it up for all to see. You then sing the second verse dealing with number "2." Use the last four measures of the song to improvise directions until the numbers are in correct sequence. When this has been done with number "1" and "2," sing the third verse and the numbers can "trade" places back and forth until the proper sequence is established. This is the game portion of the activity, and the children will delight in watching the "numbers" trade places in line with each other until they are properly assembled.

As the children become familiar with the song and the game connected with it, it will not be long before they know it well enough to take turns being the teacher in directing the "numbers" to their proper sequence. From this activity it is hoped that children will learn not only what numbers look like but also how to place them in order from one through ten.

Counting and Listening

Another activity to give young children experience in counting and assist them in becoming more discrete listeners requires a minimum of materials—one set of resonator bells or a piano.

Ask the children to count out loud "1-2-3" several times. This will familiarize them with the order and cadence of saying this

NUMBERS IN A LINE*
A number recognition song

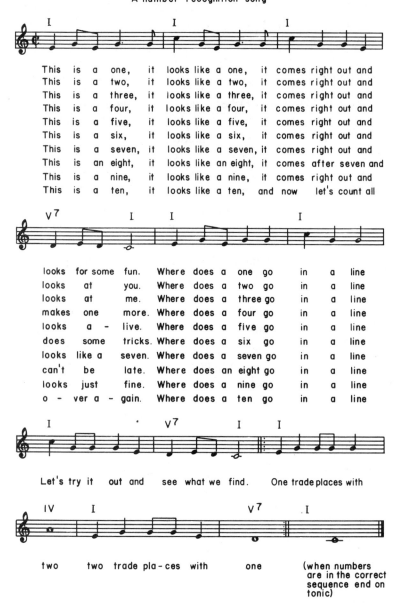

This   is   a   one,   it   looks like a   one,   it   comes right out and
This   is   a   two,   it   looks like a   two,   it   comes right out and
This   is   a   three,   it   looks like a   three,   it   comes right out and
This   is   a   four,   it   looks like a   four,   it   comes right out and
This   is   a   five,   it   looks like a   five,   it   comes right out and
This   is   a   six,   it   looks like a   six,   it   comes right out and
This   is   a   seven,   it   looks like a   seven,   it   comes right out and
This   is   an   eight,   it   looks like an eight,   it   comes after seven and
This   is   a   nine,   it   looks like a   nine,   it   comes right out and
This   is   a   ten,   it   looks like a   ten,   and   now   let's count all

looks   for some   fun.   Where   does a   one   go   in   a   line
looks   at   you.   Where   does a   two   go   in   a   line
looks   at   me.   Where   does a   three go   in   a   line
makes   one   more.   Where   does a   four   go   in   a   line
looks   a -   live.   Where   does a   five   go   in   a   line
does   some   tricks.   Where   does a   six   go   in   a   line
looks   like a   seven.   Where   does a   seven go   in   a   line
can't   be   late.   Where   does an   eight go   in   a   line
looks   just   fine.   Where   does a   nine   go   in   a   line
o -   ver a - gain.   Where   does a   ten   go   in   a   line

Let's try it   out and   see what we   find.   One trade places with

two   two   trade pla - ces   with   one   (when numbers
                                                 are in the correct
                                                 sequence end on
                                                 tonic)

Figure 3-2

* Song composed by students in Dr. Batcheller's class in Music for Early
Childhood at the University of New Mexico.

number sequence. Then, ask him to count *silently* and listen as you play three different pitches on whatever instrument is available in the classroom. Finally, ask the children to count again silently "1-2-3" and listen, for the pitches will be different. Play the same three-pitch pattern, but change the pitch of one of the numbers. The children will respond by telling which number they heard that was different. Gradually extend the pattern to 1-2-3-4 and 1-2-3-4-5, etc. As the class becomes adept, try changing two numbers and perhaps even three numbers. How far you go with this depends on the level of interest the activity generates and the pitch abilities of your particular group of children.

> NOTE: This activity is a valuable way of directing children to focus and develop their pitch awareness as well as giving them many opportunities to count in a sequential order.

BUILDING LANGUAGE AWARENESS

It is never too early for a child to become familiar with his language. This includes how the language looks as well as how it sounds. In order to help bring visual awareness of letters to young children, they should be given opportunities such as the following activities provide to explore the appearance of these letters.

Vowels and Consonants

For this activity, print each child's first name on a 10″ x 3″ piece of cardboard using two different colors, one color for consonants and another for vowels. In this way, the children can easily distinguish which letters are vowels, which consonants. Punch holes at the top upper left and right ends of the printed cardboard nametags, then attach cord through the holes and tie it so the tags can be hung around each child's neck, with his printed name facing out at chest level (see Figure 3-3).

Figure 3-3   Nametags

From here, there are several ways this activity can go. One way is to have all the children with three-letter names such as Dot, Ben and Ada form a circle facing center. They can either sit on chairs or sit cross-legged on the floor. In this manner they can all see each other's nametags. Next, start a clapping rhythm in 3's accenting the first beat and continue until all the children feel and clap a steady rhythm. This alone is an excellent activity for creating an ensemble feeling for a steady rhythm. Once they are sensing the ensemble with clapping and accenting, have them all look at the first child and clap and spell aloud the name on his nametag. Direct their action by pointing to each letter as the class spells and claps. Finally, invite the group to spell and clap on letters of one color and slap their thighs and spell the letters of the other color. This will require greater concentration and it can be expected that many attempts will be necessary as the children strive toward perfection. It is during these attempts, which should always be conducted in the spirit of fun, that learning is taking place. While the boys and girls are watching the nametags and trying to coordinate clapping and thigh-slapping, they are experiencing a close relationship with letters.

The final part of this activity is an important one from a musical standpoint. However, before this is attempted, the children should be able to accomplish what has been described so they can give their full attention to the music. A fine recording of a moderately slow, steady waltz such as the famous one from "The Damnation of Faust" by Hector Berlioz should be played. Once the children sense the 3 rhythm, they may begin going around the circle clapping and slapping the letters on each nametag in time with the recorded waltz. A game can be played by having a child drop out of the circle when that child makes an error until the players are reduced to the last child who is declared the winner.

The children with four-letter first names can form a circle and proceed the same way. When they have acquired the skill of clapping and slapping steady beats, a recording with an easy, moderately slow 4 rhythm such as J. S. Bach's "Brandenburg Concerto #1 in F Major" should be played. Here, as before, the children will clap and slap in time with the music.

Eventually, when the children become proficient at this activity, those with three-letter names and those with four-letter names can mix in circles with children having even longer names. When this occurs, a recording of a strong march such as Sousa's "Washington Post" or the familiar "Colonel Bogey" should be played. The activity then proceeds with the boys and girls clapping and slapping each other's names on the steady beats of the chosen march.

Eye Span

When children learn to read the printed word they are often troubled when they lose their place on the page. This difficulty has much to do with eye span and that special kind of rhythm that carries their eyes from left to right and back again. Children need many experiences in this kind of activity before they are competent to begin the actual process of reading. The following offers one activity that helps boys and girls achieve greater agility and accuracy with eye span and, at the same time, can be incorporated with their growing awareness of rhythm.

To prepare for this activity, make a chart from a plastic or canvas window shade (or butcher's paper) 52 inches long and whatever width is needed to accommodate the number of rows used in the activity (see the sample in Figure 3-4). Across the top of the chart, print numbers from 1 through 12 in large type. Along the left margin, print the letters A, B, C, and D in large type. Draw lines in black to establish squares made by the letters and numbers.

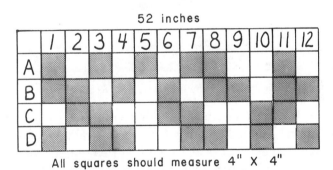

All squares should measure 4" X 4"

Figure 3-4 Suggested Eye-span Chart

NOTE: The numbers represent beats in the music and the letters guide children in reading from line to line. Twelve beats are used in order to include most conventional meter signatures.

Finally, paint various squares with a solid color. Use one color throughout. (When a square is colored, the children will clap or play a drum on that particular beat.)

Begin this activity by having the children count out loud with you from 1 through 12 over and over until a steady cadence of moderate speed is attained. Then, beginning at Row A, with the command of, "Ready, clap" or "Ready, play," have the children clap or play the drum on the square that is colored and do nothing (rest) on the squares that are blank. At the end of Row A the children must return to Row B and respond to those squares and finally finish with Rows C and D. It is important that they understand they must go directly from the last beat (12) of the first row (A) to the first beat (1) of the second row (B) without losing the cadence. The strength and life of the rhythm should carry them along and force them to adjust their sight to the next row. More rows can be added from time to time as well as many different rhythm patterns.

When the children have grasped what is expected of them, select an appropriate recording of moderate speed and have them clap or play along with it from the colored squares on the chart.

Variations on this idea might consist of using a different color for each row (see Figure 3-5). Have one group of children with

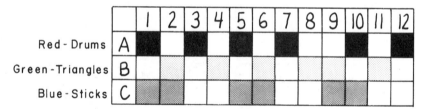

Figure 3-5   Rhythmic Texture Eye Span

drums read Row A (red) while another group with triangles read Row B (green) and still another group holds rhythm sticks ready Row C (blue). This creates an interesting rhythmic texture as well as fosters independence among the players along with eye-span movement.

SHAPE RECOGNITION

Activities such as the following are among the favorites of children who have experienced them. Try each phase of this activity with this reassurance in mind: Always be prepared to simplify any aspect and to accommodate it to the limitations of your own class-room. For example, if you cannot obtain sufficient elastic rope, or if you do not have a large space for movement, be prepared to use fewer materials, and fewer children, moving by turns.

Elastic Ropes

This activity necessitates finding heavy elastic banding in a dry goods store. Obtain sixty feet of the elastic rope and cut it into six-foot lengths. Sew each end together securely to form a ring. This amount of elastic will make ten ropes. If more ropes are needed, increase the original amount by multiples of six feet for each additional rope. Try to confine the group in this activity to ten or under. Very young children have a strong tendency to get out of hand with these elastic ropes when they operate in larger groups.

First, invite the children to explore the elastic ropes by pulling them apart with both arms out as far as possible and then slowly allowing the ropes to resume their original shapes (see Figure 3-6, Position A). Never allow any snapping or slingshot kind of behavior. Next, have the children stand in one side of the rope with both feet while they pull the other side of the rope over their heads with both hands (Position B). Here, they end up standing inside the elastic rope, which outlines a shape created by both of their hands and feet. While the boys and girls are in this position, have them slowly raise one foot from the floor and place all their body weight on the other foot. This maneuver should be done slowly with the tension of the elastic rope felt on both hands and both feet (Position C). It can be seen that this activity leads toward the development of balance and body coordination.

When the children have had sufficient time to discover the many possibilities involving ways they can manipulate these elastic ropes, ask them to get into a starting position—standing in one side of the rope with both feet about a foot apart and holding the other end of the rope with both hands just until the tension in the elastic is felt (Position D). Next, ask them to listen to the music you will play and to follow your verbal directions. Slow, relaxing music with soft dynamics should be used to create mood and allow your voice to be heard above the sound without having to shout. Erik Satie's "Gymnopedie #3" (Columbia M30294) and Mozart's "Piano Concerto in C Major," second movement (Turnabout #34800) are

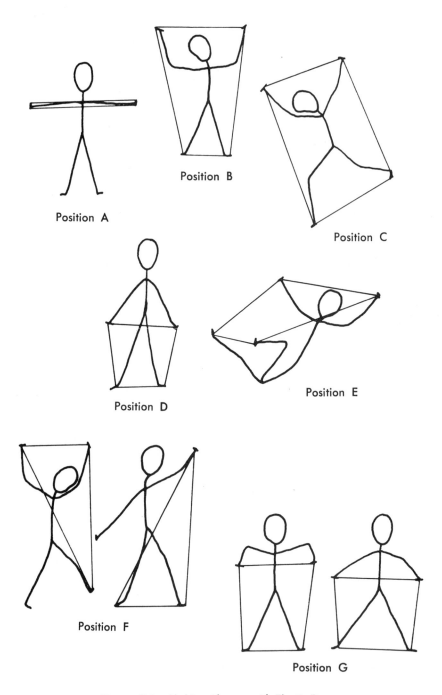

Position A

Position B

Position C

Position D

Position E

Position F

Position G

Figure 3-6 Making Shapes with Elastic Ropes

both excellent selections to use for this activity. The following verbal directions are an example of how a teacher might guide a group of children as they move through this activity with their elastic ropes.

(Begin recording and let it play for about a full minute to set the mood.)

Teacher: Everyone listen to the music. Now, very slowly, raise your right arm as high as you can reach . . . slowly . . . very slowly. Do you feel the tension or pull in the elastic rope? Now, slowly raise your right foot but be sure you do not let the rope pull away from it. Try to keep your balance as you move very slowly. Let the music tell you how to move. Next, slowly place your right foot back on the floor ahead of your left foot. As soon as your feet are both on the floor, bring your left hand holding the rope up to your right hand. Remember, you are listening carefully to the music and it is telling you to move slowly. Now, bend backward with your body. Don't tip over! Try to keep your balance. Slowly try to open your arms now and begin to lower them very, very slowly . . . don't rush! Bring them lower in front of your head still holding the rope. Can you bend your body over so your hands can touch each of your feet? Good . . . now straighten up your body and bring both hands way over to the left while you pull the tension on the rope . . . slowly . . . [etc.].

It should be noted how many times in the activity a child comes in contact with directional words such as left-right, high-low, forward-backward, and so on. Once the idea of this activity is clearly understood, invite the child to create whatever shapes and whatever movements reflect his feelings about the music he is hearing. Eventually, two children can manipulate the same elastic rope. This kind of an experience allows the children to become aware of each other's feelings and desires while experiencing a sense of teamwork to achieve common goals.

For teachers interested in giving young children experiences in movement that will develop their physical coordination, it must be emphasized that this activity with elastic ropes should become almost a daily function. Only through frequent exposure to this type of movement will body balance and coordination become realities in the classroom.

One teacher remarked, "We have movement on Friday." Here is a school's philosophy exposed for what it is. A school answering the immediate developmental needs of very young children will offer *daily* opportunities in which they can experience and discover the grace and beauty of their own bodies. In this activity, the tension of the elastic ropes and the feeling aroused by the music combine to guide children toward an esthetic response and controlled movement.

An interesting way to connect this activity with the recognition of basic geometric shapes is first to show children large cut-out forms of different sizes of squares, triangles and rectangles. Let the children trace the outlines of these forms with their fingers. The shapes can be attached to a display board or placed on the floor. You should designate the difference between the square and a rectangle and a triangle. Considerable discussion is beneficial at this point. When the children can identify a shape accurately, they are ready to "become" that shape with their elastic ropes.

Next, ask the children to step into their elastic ropes and with their two hands and feet outline a square, then a rectangle, and finally a triangle. Very young children will need assistance until they grasp what is expected of them. They learn much faster from watching each other in this respect than being manipulated by the teacher. Therefore, it is helpful to have them create these shapes in pairs facing each other. After they have outlined a shape one way, ask them to find another way to make that same shape—perhaps a larger or smaller square, a triangle with the base above their heads and the apex on the floor held down with one foot, a rectangle with longer or shorter corresponding sides. Some children will want to create these shapes from a sitting position and this should certainly be encouraged (Positions E, F, G). Soon the children should be able to create these basic shapes with very little difficulty. When this time is reached, you can then put this activity to music and make a delightful game of it.

One way of doing this is to obtain a recording of Richard Strauss' "Also Sprach Zarathustra." The Columbia recording #M30443 conducted by Leonard Bernstein is highly recommended. Upon listening to this recording, the teacher will discover the first few moments of the composition consist of three exciting crescendi (the music gradually becomes louder). Each of these crescendi is followed by a thrilling sforzando (a sudden loud attack). It is advisable to play the beginning of this recording several times to become familiar with the time of these three places in the music because during these moments you will give instructions to the children.

The activity begins with the boys and girls stepping into their elastic ropes and grasping the opposite ends of them with their hands

(Position D). Then, start the recording and, while the first crescendo begins to build, explain to the class that they are to create the shape you announce as soon as they hear a great orchestral crash in the music. After a few trials, you will be able to synchronize your command, "Be a square!" or "Be a triangle!" or "Be a rectangle!" with the sforzando attack in the music. The music is so moving at these attack points it all but lifts the children into becoming the various shapes. Their delight and excitement is most apparent. For this activity, use only this short portion of the Strauss work. After the third attack is experienced, the recording can be repeated from the beginning. By doing this, each time the work is played the class will become involved in creating three geometric shapes. Of course, other commands can be given to vary the activity and to suit whatever the class is interested in doing.

DEVELOPING A POSITIVE SELF-IMAGE

Throughout early childhood, you will notice the stages of musical awareness and sensitivity grow and develop if you look for positive ways to reward and encourage involvement. Each child wants to be recognized for who and what he is—a person with capabilities and personhood.

Encouraging Personal Response

At almost every point within a music program, try to ask questions that children must answer from their storehouse of experiences. These may appear to be simple ways of gaining a response, but this type of personal treatment during the early days of a child's life will never be wasted. The following list of suggested questions will give you some clues as to others you can add on your own.

- "What is your favorite song of all the songs we have sung in class? Why do you choose that one?"
- "How would you move your hands to show you are happy?"
- "Which of these two sounds make you think of chocolate candy? Why did you select that one?"
- "In the morning when you get out of bed which describes best how you feel—a violin or a tuba? Can you tell why?
- "Does the rhythm I will play on this drum remind you of day or night? What about it makes you feel that way?"
- "Which is the youngest of these three sounds? Why?"

- "How would you be a dangerous volcano without making any sounds?"
- "Tell a story on the bells about catching a falling star."
- "Make two different sounds on the autoharp. Can you explain why one is more beautiful than the other to you?"

Almost any child would be able to respond somehow to these questions. The unique thing about a child's response is that whatever it may be, it will be correct and very personal to that child. It is the teacher's role to let the child know that his response is something "special." When you succeed in doing this, a child feels a sense of pride and his self-image grows another inch. To be sure, a child can be made to feel somewhat important when he spells a word accurately or satisfactorily adds 2 plus 1. If his responses here are correct, they will be just like those of every other child's correct responses. In being merely correct, the golden uniqueness of a child's response fades into a grey sameness. In this important area of reaching children and enriching their self-esteem, music can indeed prove most rewarding.

Consider the first question, inquiring of the child what song he likes best. This is a very intimate domain because singing involves so much of one's personality. A teacher might expect anything in response to the question and when a child explains why a certain song was chosen by him, he reveals more and more of his own uniqueness. Therefore, it is imperative that his response be treated with respect and consideration.

Stimulating Individualism

In addition to encouraging response to questions, you should develop ways to encourage children to express their individuality while reinforcing them with meaningful compliments. The following statements can serve to guide you in recognizing and commenting on the musical expressions of children:

- "Billy has a wonderful idea of how to move like a volcano. Show it to all of us Billy."
- "How many can guess what Peg is telling us on the bells?"
- "If Howard and Beth would hold the screen in front of everyone, June will show us what she has done with her hand puppets."
- "Jim has a great story to tell us in movement."
- "Listen to how musically Ted can make his drum talk."
- "Lois is showing happiness with her hand movements in a way I've never seen before."

- "Sally would like to send us some musical messages with her hands. See how many you can understand."
- "Carl, tell us why you feel like a tuba when you first get up in the morning."
- "Carla just told me why she feels the autoharp sounds beautiful when she plays it this way. It is such a good reason, I want her to share it with you."
- "Al said the rhythm reminded him of nighttime and so did Debbie. Let's hear if they have different reasons."
- "Did you all hear how Inez changed the ending of the song? I think it's better that way. Sing it your way for us again Inez."

Each of the preceding statements places the individual child in a positive light before his peers. Each, in some small way, attempts to bring all children together in a more intimate manner. Through these modest responses and experiences, the teacher and the children are able to nurture relationships that allow each person to become known and admired for his or her own personal, special attributes, opinions and choices. Thus, each child is better able to discover more of his own personal worth. This worth might be enhanced when a child finds he is the first one to master the skill of skipping in time to a recording, being able to join two others and clap a steady rhythm, designate the difference between a high sound and a low sound, add an original rhythm on a drum to a song the class is singing, describe beauty as only he sees and feels it. This idea is reflected in the following anonymous poem.

> Music is a child's way of saying——
>   "I'm an individual, can't you tell?
> And though you may not know it
>   I think I sing pretty well.
> It may not sound so good
>   And it may not be on key——
> But the most important thing
>   Is that the sound is coming from me.
> At reading and numbers I'm not so great,
>   As I'm sure you can plainly see.
> But when it comes to music . . .
>   Teacher, you can count on me!"
> So let this child feel successful,
>   Though he can't do everything——
> And you'll know he feels better about himself,
>   'Cause teacher—you let him sing!

4

Music Interest Centers

Many primary classrooms now include interest centers. In these areas, children can browse through materials relating to different activities within the total curriculum. In one corner of the classroom, there might be a reading nook where boys and girls can browse through books, play word games, or match pictures with words. In another location, it is not uncommon to find a tank of tropical fish, a pair of hamsters exercising in their treadwheel, a cage of gerbils, or seeds germinating in see-through containers. Here, children can observe, at leisure, the phenomena of science, nature, and biology. Music, too, is an appropriate subject for the creation of an exciting interest center in the primary instructional area.

STARTING A CLASSROOM MUSIC CENTER

A simple beginning for a classroom music center can be made by partitioning off a corner of the classroom from the rest of the room by a small upright piano or shoulder-high bookcase. If a piano is used, make certain the back of the instrument is facing the outside area so that the keyboard is part of the interest center. In this way a small 8′ x 10′ space with two solid walls and an opening could be created (see Figure 4-1). One of the walls should be used as a display board. Here, you can display pictorial materials pertaining to various aspects of music such as: pictures of musical instruments, children dancing, children's "music" art work, candid snapshots of the children themselves involved in musical activities, programs, illustrations depicting native musicians playing ethnic instruments from many parts of the world. In short, you should attempt to make this display wall a dramatic feature that, hopefully, will elicit comments and questions from the children.

On the other wall, attach a chalkboard on which children can react to whatever is happening with music. Here, a child can represent the shape of a melody, highs and lows with regard to pitches,

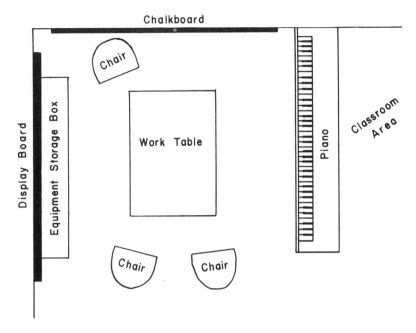

Figure 4-1   Suggested Floor Plan for a Music Interest Center

accents, how duple and triple rhythms might appear if one were to draw them. A chalkboard could be important and will probably be put to daily use.

It is a good idea to place a low table and three or four small chairs in the center of this area. On the table, phonographic and recording equipment can be placed for immediate and convenient use. If cassettes are used with listening earphones, here is the ideal location—amid musical surroundings! When musical games are played by two or three children, this provides a secluded spot for them. Somewhere in the area a large box or low bookcase should contain rhythm instruments for easy access and storage.

Using the Interest Center

How children use this area depends on the attitude of the teacher toward their creative instincts and curiosity. An example of how one teacher used the center resulted from a boy wandering in one day and running his hand down the length of the piano keyboard and then dashing outside and hiding. Inadvertently, the teacher found him and casually asked if he enjoyed the sound he created on the piano and if he would like to do it again. He responded positively and went with the teacher into the music center where he again ran his hand the length of the keyboard. The teacher then produced a small diatonic xylophone and asked the boy to take a mallet and do the same thing on the xylophone that he had done on the piano. He did this with great zeal. The teacher explained that what he had done was called a "glissando" and asked him to say the word several times to enjoy the "feel" of it. The sibilant sounds were fascinating. At this point the boy appeared relaxed and full of wonder at what he had discovered and when invited to bring two of his friends back to the music center to share his new word, he became eager and excited to do so.

Another teacher placed five glass bottles filled with different levels of colored water on the table in the music center. She hoped that some children would discover them. Soon, two girls sought her out to inquire what the bottles were for. This was a starting point for an interesting exploration of pitches and an awareness of high and low tones. The girls became so interested they spread the word to other children, playing the role of the teacher as they, in turn, explained what the teacher had told them.

In both of these instances, the "tools" for a musical experience were simply there, and the teacher capitalized on the natural curiosity of children to instigate a meaningful response.

The Music Store

An interesting modification of the music interest center is a "Music Store" with merchandise display counters where the children can place all the soundmakers they created complete with price tags. The prices can be arrived at through discussion with the teacher and those children who are acting as store "personnel." In this way, a very real association with values might be experienced. If some specific kind of musical merchandise is needed, the store personnel can contract with any of the children to make it or find it. Ideas of what this sound merchandise might consist of are:

> Expensive High Sounds
> Big-money Low Sounds
> Super-savings Scraping Sounds
> Elaborate Scraping Sounds
> Executive Heavy Sounds

Top-quality Light Sounds
Exclusive Clicking Sounds
Unusual Smooth Sounds
Graveyard-tested Spooky Sounds
Inexpensive High Sounds
Cut-rate Low Sounds
Discount Heavy Sounds
Economy Light Sounds
Everyday Clicking Sounds
Standard Sleepy Sounds

Children should come up with their own ideas rather than making and collecting prescribed items that were the thoughts of others. This will allow for creative development in selecting and rating each sound item in the store.

When the various items have been priced, marked and displayed, children can create money from different-colored cardboard discs, as shown in Figure 4-2. From here the possibilities of building

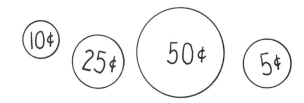

Figure 4-2

relationships are numerous, i.e., the store, the musical merchandise, the play money, value concepts, mathematical concepts, and musical ideas. Interesting experiences are limited only by the teacher's imagination.

For example, one teacher found that the music store was an excellent setting that allowed her class to be creative in choice and have experience "shopping." After her class had learned to sing "Ancona Chicken," she asked what two different sounds could be added that would make the song more interesting when the class sang it. The teacher asked two children to browse in the music store for ideas and come back to the group with suggestions. This they did. When it was finally decided which two sounds would be used, another child volunteered to go to the "bank" and draw out enough money to buy these sounds at the store and make the desired purchases.

In another situation, a teacher asked a child to select a 5-cent "sound" to go with "Hickory Dickory Dock" or a 25-cent scary sound to use with a new Halloween song. The possibilities can easily be seen, but it should be cautioned, the music interest center should not be abolished in favor of the music store idea. Rather, the music store might be a changing part of the center, even disappearing altogether from time to time.

MANIPULATIVE OBJECTS

Children enjoy looking at things and handling various objects. Through these explorations, they come to know how things feel and how they work. Much of their naive curiosity is satisfied in this manner and it is through these "looking" and "touching" experiences that learning can actually take place.

Successful teaching should produce questions like these:

- What is it?
- Can I play with it?
- How does it work?
- What is it supposed to be?
- Does it make a sound?
- Can I show it to Charles?
- What's it for?
- What does it do?
- Can I make one?
- Will you tell me about it?

In order to elicit these kinds of questions, the learning environment should include many material motivators. These can take the form of interesting "fun" games, objects the children can manipulate, and other items that are merely a delight to have around and observe.

An excellent location for these items would, of course, be the music interest center. Here, on display boards, shelves, and tables, you can arrange different objects that will focus on whatever concept or skill is being explored. Following are directions for making a number of simple, easy-to-construct manipulative items.

Communications Column

A Communications Column is a cardboard column about

twenty inches high with five-inch sides. It serves as an excellent aid in exploring different ways to communicate through music.

To make a Communications Column, all you will need are a cardboard box about 20″ x 5″ x 5″ and a black felt-tipped marker. On one side of the column, print numbers from 1 through 8 from the bottom up. On another side, print the singing syllables (Do, Re, Mi, etc.), and on another side draw the Kodaly hand signals. Leave the fourth side blank for the children to create a system of their own if they so desire.

Place the Communications Column in a conspicuous spot in the music interest center where children can see immediate comparisons as well as observe numbers and syllables in their proper sequential order.

Miniature Keyboards

Many interesting, simple manipulative aids can be created with wooden bar stirrers and tongue depressors. One such aid can show musical steps and half steps, as shown in Figure 4-3. To construct this, simply glue eight tongue depressors together and onto a couple of stirrer backings. Next, glue smaller stirrers that have been painted black where they would appear to simulate a piano keyboard. Then print letter names on the depressors.

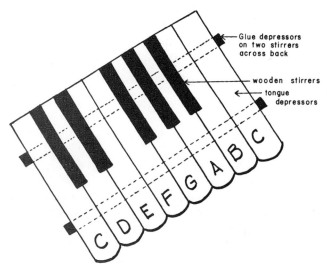

Figure 4-3   Tongue Depressor-Stirrer Keyboard

Children can become actively involved in assisting the teacher in making these miniature keyboards. Using these aids, children can discover groups of two and three black keys, the number of different sounds (notes) between two letter names, and the correct letter sequence in the musical alphabet.

NOTE: To introduce older children to different modes and movable *Do,* several of these small keyboards can be made to represent whatever mode is being studied.

Sound Makers

Here is another idea using just tongue depressors that can help children become more aware of pitches. Place a tongue depressor on a table or desk with half of it projecting over the edge and hold it tightly with one hand (Figure 4-4). With the other hand, pluck the

Figure 4-4

Making Sounds

with Tongue Depressors

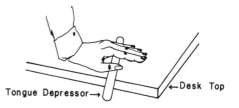

Tongue Depressor→   ←Desk Top

protruding end of the tongue depressor to create a sound. The more of the depressor that extends from the table's edge, the lower the pitch; the less that extends, the higher the pitch when plucked.

The possibilities for using these simple sound-makers are unlimited. Here are just a few suggestions as starters:

- Eight children can produce a diatonic scale—one child plucking one tone.
- Five children can produce a pentatonic scale—one child plucking one tone.
- Repeated melodic patterns (ostenati) can be created to accompany pentatonic songs.
- High, low, soft, and loud sounds can be created and identified.
- Harmonic effects can be achieved by creating an I chord and a V^7 chord using three children on each chord, each child plucking one of the triad's members.
- Rhythmic effects can be created to enrich a singing experience.
- Simple songs like "Hot Cross Buns" and "Oh How Lovely Is the Evening" can be played by several children representing the

tones in the songs. This is a good activity to assist children in developing a musical memory.

GAMES

Children learn through playing games and competing with each other. In the field of music, there are many facets that adapt easily to this kind of creative learning. Here is one easy-to-make game that might be included in the music interest center.

Fish Pond

Materials

To make this game, you will need the following materials and tools:

3′ x 2′ cardboard box
Enough blue construction paper to cover the outside of the box
Three ⅜″ diameter 3-foot wooden doweling poles
Small pieces of different-colored construction paper
Metal staples
3 small magnets
9 feet of nylon cord (thread)
Scissors
Paste
Felt-tipped marker

Construction

Directions for constructing the game are as follows:

1. Cover the cardboard box with blue paper and call it a "fish pond."
2. Cut out many fish forms from the colored, lightweight paper, and place a metal staple near the fish's mouth, as shown in Figure 4-5.
3. On each fish, write something to do with regard to music. For example:

- Identify 𝅘𝅥

- Sing three pitches and tell which one was the highest

- Identify

- Sing "This Old Man"
- Identify ♩
- Recite in rhythm
- Identify ♪
- Beat the drum in an even steady manner to the count of 12
- Sing "Hot Cross Buns"
- Identify (picture of a trombone)

4. Finally, make three-foot fishing poles out of the ⅜″ doweling. Attach a piece of nylon thread with a magnet tied to the end of each pole. (The small magnets can be purchased in hardware stores, hobby shops, and some variety stores.)

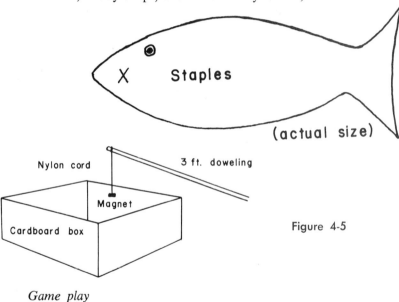

Game play

It is best to limit the number of players in this game to two or three children, because interest lags when each child must wait too long for his turn.

The game is played by having one child "fish" in the box where all the fish have been placed. When the magnet at the end of the child's line has made contact with the metal staple on the fish's mouth, the child pulls in the fish and attempts to do what his "catch" demands. If he succeeds, he earns a point. After five rounds, the winner is determined by the greatest number of successful attempts.

5

Individualized Music Lessons

Much emphasis is being placed on individualized instruction today. What could be more personal than specially prepared tapes with specific boys and girls in mind? Teaching children in their early years certain basic concepts to be discovered in music—high/low, fast/slow, loud/soft, even/uneven, steps/skips—can easily and enjoyably be accomplished by using taped lessons. Knowing her children, a teacher can prepare a five-to-eight-minute lesson, record it on a cassette tape, and invite one or two children to listen to it. These children, in turn, can tell their friends about it, and soon many children in the class will have been personally exposed to some interesting facet of music.

This section presents guidelines for making your own individualized taped lessons plus two complete sample lessons for teaching concepts of fast and slow, upward-downward and steps-skips.

GUIDELINES FOR MAKING A TAPE

The following are some suggestions that should help insure the most effective presentation and use of taped lessons:

1. Use short tapes and begin to develop a bank of taped lessons. Once a lesson is taped, you have it forever and can begin to create a new one. Think of the time this saves in open education!
2. Select an objective for each tape commensurate with the age of children. This is important!
3. Decide how you want to present the objective of the lesson.
4. Write a scenario and time it. For very young children, try to stay within the five-to-seven-minute range. Lessons for older children might take up to ten minutes.
5. Tell children on the tape what the lesson is all about—present the lesson—then tell them what has happened.
6. Speak slowly and distinctly but do not talk "down" to the children.
7. Attempt to involve the children in some physical manner.

NOTE: *Just listening is not good!* Use innovative devices to capture the children's interest. Ask them to make unique responses.

8. Try to end the taped lesson with some kind of evaluation device so that the children and you can see if the experience has been successful.
9. Invite children to play the tape again or to play it for a friend.

LESSON: CONCEPTS OF FAST AND SLOW

Here is a sample lesson attempting to acquaint preschoolers with the concept of fast and slow in music.

Teacher: You are going to hear several pieces of music. Some of the music you will hear will move slowly and some will move quickly. While you are listening, decide whether the music moves quickly or slowly. If you feel it moves slowly, sway back and forth with your body, but if you feel the music moves quickly, shake your fingers in the air with both hands. Remember, you sway your body if the music is slow or shake your fingers in the air if the music is fast.
Ready? Listen!

[Record fifteen seconds of a very slow excerpt]

Teacher: Did you sway your body back and forth? I hope so because that was a slow piece of music, wasn't it?
Now, listen again and do what the music tells you to do.

[Record fifteen seconds of a very fast excerpt]

Teacher: Did you shake your fingers in front of you? That was a fast piece of music, wasn't it?
Now, try this next one and see what it tells you to do. This time either sway your body or shake your fingers in time with the music. It's really more fun that way.

[Record fifteen seconds of a very fast excerpt. During the last five seconds speak over the recording and continue playing it for another ten seconds.]

Teacher: I hope you are shaking your fingers in time with the music. This is a fast one, isn't it?
Let's try one more. Listen carefully!

[Record fifteen seconds of a very slow excerpt]

Teacher: Did you sway your body back and forth? That was a slow piece of music like the first one you heard.

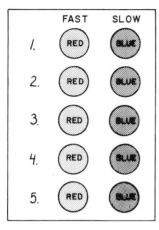

Figure 5-1 Sample Score Card
for Cassette Lesson

For the very young, colored circles are used instead of words. The teacher may find it necessary to guide the children until they understand what is expected of them.

Now, look at the score card in front of you. We are going to play a little game with it. [See Figure 5-1]
You will see numbers from one to five. After each number is a red circle and a blue circle. When you hear me say, "Number one," take your pencil and make a big check mark right across the red circle if the music you hear is fast, but if you feel it is slow, make your check mark across the blue circle. Remember, check the red circle for fast music and the blue circle for slow music. Then you will hear me say, "Number two," followed by more music until you have had all five turns.
Ready? Here we go.

Number one . . . . [Play fifteen seconds of fast music]
Number two . . . . [Fifteen seconds of slow music]
Number three . . . . . [Fifteen seconds of slow music]
Number four . . . . . . [Fifteen seconds of fast music]
Number five . . . . [Fifteen seconds of fast music]

Now check with me and see what score you made. Number one was fast so you should have checked the red circle. Number two was slow and you should have checked the blue circle. Number three was also slow and another check mark on the blue circle. Number four was fast so see if you checked the red circle. Number five was also a fast piece, so you should have checked the red circle there. Did you get them all? If not, rewind the tape and listen again.

LESSON: CONCEPTS OF UPWARD-DOWNWARD; STEPS-SKIPS

The following individualized lesson is an example of what one teacher prerecorded with very simple musical examples played on

a piano or set of resonator bells. This lesson was created for eight-
or nine-year-olds.

Teacher: Let's talk about melody. Melodies are several notes strung together
that produce a tune. Melodies can move in different ways. Here is a short
melody that moves upward by skips.

Pattern #1
Example of a Melody
Moving Upward by Skips

[Play Pattern #1]

Listen to it once again.

[Repeat Pattern #1]

Listen once more and show the direction of the melody going upward by
skips with your hand. Remember to make enough space between the notes
of the melody to show the skips.

[Repeat Pattern #1]

Now, here is a melody that also moves upward, only this time it moves by
steps. Listen.

Pattern #2
Example of a Melody
Moving Upward by Steps

[Play Pattern #2]

Did you hear five notes in that melody? Listen again and move your hand
in front of you to show the melody moving upward by steps.

[Repeat Pattern #2]

You have heard two ways a melody can move. One way was going upward
by skips.

[Repeat Pattern #1]

The second way you heard was the melody going upward by steps.

[Repeat Pattern #2]

Did you hear the difference?
Next, listen to this melody. It moves still another way. This time it moves
downward by skips.

Pattern #3
Example of a Melody
Moving Downward by Skips

[Play Pattern #3]

Listen again and show how it moves with your hand. Remember, it is moving downward by skips.

[Repeat Pattern #3]

Now, listen to the melody move another way.

Pattern #4
Example of a Melody
Moving Downward by Steps

[Play Pattern #4]

How did you hear the melody move that time? If you heard it move downward by steps, you were correct. Show how it moves downward by steps with your hand as it is repeated for you.

[Repeat Pattern #4]

Now, let's reveiw the four ways a melody can move. First, it can move upward by skips.

[Repeat Pattern #1]

Then it can move upward by steps.

[Repeat Pattern #2]

The third way we heard the melody move was downward by skips.

[Repeat Pattern #3]

And the fourth way a melody can move is downward by steps. Listen.

[Repeat Pattern #4]

Longer melodies combine these ways to make them sound more interesting. Listen to this melody and hear if you can discover the two ways it moves.

Pattern #5   Example of a Melody Combining Moving Upward by Skips
and Moving Downward by Steps

[Play Pattern #5]

Listen to it once again.

[Repeat Pattern #5]

Did you hear it begin by moving upward by skips and then turn around and move downward by steps? If you did, you were correct.

Now, take your score card and a pencil. [See Figure 5-2]

SCORE CARD				
MELODY	UPWARD	DOWNWARD	SKIPS	STEPS
1				
2				
3				
4				
5				

Figure 5-2

You are going to hear each melody twice. The first time you hear it place an X in whichever column you think it moves—upward or downward. The second time you hear that same melody decide if it moves by steps or skips and place an X in whichever column you select.

Ready? Here is Melody #1.

Melody #1

[Play Melody #1]

Listen to Melody #1 again and this time check either in the skips or steps column.

[Repeat Melody #1]

Now, listen to Melody #2.

Melody #2

[Play Melody #2]

Listen again to Melody #2.

[Repeat Melody #2]

Next, listen to Melody #3.

Melody #3

[Play Melody #3]

Here is Melody #3 again.

[Repeat Melody #3]

Now, listen to Melody #4 and make the appropriate check marks.

Melody #4

[Play Melody #4]

Listen again to Melody #4.

[Repeat Melody #4]

The last one is Melody #5. Listen carefully to Melody #5.

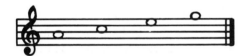

Melody #5

[Play Melody #5]

Listen again to Melody #5.

[Repeat Melody #5]

How do you think you scored? Let's find out. Go back on your score card and check your answers with me. Ready?

Melody #1 moved upward by skips.
Melody #2 moved downward by steps.
Melody #3 moved downward by skips.
Melody #4 moved upward by steps.
Melody #5 moved upward by skips.

If you ran into any trouble, go back and replay the tape and see if you can improve.

Useful Resources

This section includes books and recordings that you could use in your music program for early childhood. Because of the many publications available in this field, the following criteria were kept in mind when making selections: (1) easy-to-use materials that are adaptable to a variety of programs and philosophies; (2) currently available resources that are not overly expensive and can be ordered with a minimum of difficulty; and (3) materials that have been effectively used with children.

The materials selected are organized into three main subsections: Teacher References, Song and Game Books, and Recordings for Singing and Moving. Finally, there is a brief listing of basic music series titles and publishers.

TEACHER REFERENCES

Aronoff, Frances Webber, *Music and Young Children*. (New York: Holt-Rinehart, Winston, Inc., 1969.) Handbook for music in early childhood. Comprehensive and well-researched.

Beer, Alice, and Mary Hoffman, *Teaching Music, What, How, Why*. (Morristown, New Jersey: General Learning Press, 1973.) Excellent overall book including ideas for individualizing instruction in music.

Bergethon, Bjornar, and Eunice Boardman, *Musical Growth in the Elementary School*. (New York: Holt, Rinehart, Winston, Inc. 1970.) Plan for a sequential music program for K–6. Good comprehensive book with many teaching ideas.

Biasini, Americole, et al., *Early Childhood Music Curriculum* (Bardonia; New York: Media Materials, Inc., 1972.)

Commins, Dorothy Berliner, *Lullabies of the World*. (New York: Random House, Inc., 1967.) A rare collection of folk lullabies from around the world, each presented in its native tongue and translated into English.

Dallin, Leon, and Lynn Dallin, *Folk Songster. Heritage Songster*. (Dubuque, Iowa: Wm. C. Brown Pub., 1972.) Comprehensive collection of folk songs with original languages and English. Information about the songs included.

Greenberg, Marvin, and Beatrix MacGregor, *Music Handbook for the Elementary School*. (West Nyack, N.Y.: Parker Publishing Company, Inc., 1972.) A comprehensive practical manual for planning and teaching elementary music.

Hood, Marguerite, *Teaching Rhythm and Using Classroom Instruments.* (Englewood Cliffs, N.J.: Prentice-Hall, 1970.) A book with many suggestions for instrumental accompaniments, rhythmic activities, etc.

Horton, John, *Music in Informal Schools in Britain Today.* (New York: Citation Press, 1972.) Description of British "open" education programs in music.

Kersey, Robert, ed., *Just Five.* (Melville, N.Y.: Belwin Mills, 1972.) A collection of pentatonic folk melodies and other songs with only five tones in the scale.

Landeck, Beatrice, *Songs to Grow On. More Songs to Grow On.* (New York: Edward B. Marks Music Corp., 1950.) A beautiful collection of appealing and authentic folk songs for children. Suggestions for rhythmic and instrumental play are included.

————, and Elizabeth Crook, *Wake Up and Sing!* (New York: Edward B. Marks Music Corp., 1969.) Folk songs from America's grass roots with teaching suggestions.

Langstaff, John, ed., *Frog Went A-Courtin'.* (New York: Harcourt Brace Jovanovich, 1955.) Picture book of this famous folk song. Includes the music.

McLaughlin, Roberta, and Lucille Wood, *Sing a Song!* (Englewood Cliffs, N.J.: Prentice-Hall, Inc., 1960.) Simple, easy-to-sing songs related to the interests of young children.

Monsour, Sally, *Music in Open Education.* (New York: The Center for Applied Research in Education, Inc., 1974.) Ideas for creative teaching in an informal learning environment.

Nash, Grace, *Music With Children.* (LaGrange, Ill.: Kitching Education, Ludwig Industries, 1966.) A series of books based on the ideas of Orff and Kodaly. Creative ideas and interesting musical materials for young childhood.

Nye, Robert, et al., *Singing with Children,* 2nd ed. (Belmont, Cal.: Wadsworth Publishing Corp., 1970.) Representative collection of elementary level songs for many occasions. Teaching objectives and suggestions included.

Palmer, Hap, *Hap Palmer Song Book.* (Freeport, L.I., N.Y.: Educational Activities Records, 1971.) Songs to go along with Palmer recordings.

Palmer, Mary, *Sound Exploration and Discovery.* (New York: The Center for Applied Research in Education, Inc., 1974.) Refreshing and creative ideas, especially in the area of composition and sound exploration.

Reynolds, Jane L., *Music Lessons You Can Teach*. (West Nyack, N.Y.: Parker Publishing Company, Inc., 1970.) Provides material for more than 200 classroom music lessons for grades 1 through 6.

Richard, Mary Helen, *The Child in Depth*. (Portola Valley, Cal.: Richards Institute of Music Education, 1969.) An early childhood approach to music that involves all aspects of musical involvement.

Schmitt, Sister Cecilia, "The Thought Life of the Young Child." *Music Educators Journal* (Dec., 1971), 22–26. A magazine article relating early childhood development to the ideas of Jean Piaget.

Sesame Street Song Books. (New York: New York Times Book Corp., 1972.) Songs taken from the TV series. Several volumes.

Smith, Betty, *Open Court Kindergarten Program*. (La Salle, Ill.: Open Court Pub., 1970.) A comprehensive song book (with recordings and teaching suggestions) for the kindergarten level.

SONG AND GAME BOOKS

Barlow, Betty, *Do It Yourself Songs*. (Delaware, Pa.: Shawnee Press, 1964.) A collection of songs that provides for adding ideas, actions, etc.

Bradley, Helen, and Jayne Gahagan, *The Child's Small World*. (Elgin, Ill.: David Cook Pub., 1967.) A sensitive search into a very young child's interests through music.

Wood, Lucille, *Primary Song Program*. (Glendale, Cal.: Bowmar Publishing Co., 1968.) Three books and eleven recordings that make up a comprehensive package in early childhood music. (Available as a set or separately.)

Zimmerman, George, *Seasons in Song*. (New York: M. Witmark, 1964.) Interesting songs for the various seasons of the year.

RECORDINGS FOR SINGING AND MOVING

Afro Rhythms, Montego Joe. Kimbo 6060.
Authentic rhythms from Africa, Cuba, Haiti, Brazil, Trinidad, and Puerto Rico, conducive to the development of creative imagination and improvisation.

American Folk Songs for Children, Pete Seeger, Folkways 7601.

American Games and Activity Songs, Pete Seeger. Folkways 7674.

Animal Folk Songs for Children, Peggy Seeger. Folkways 7551.

Animals and Circus, Bowmar BOL 51.

As Quiet As. RCA LSC 3001.

Birds, Beasts, and Little Fishes, Pete Seeger. Folkways 7610.
Fifteen old favorites—mostly nonsense songs.

Building Vocabulary, Hap Palmer. Educational Activities, Inc. AR 521.

Children's Concert at Town Hall, Pete Seeger. Harmony S11284.
"Put Your Finger in the Air," "Little Birdie," etc.

Dance, Sing and Listen, Dimension 5.

Dance, Sing and Listen Again!, Dimension 5.

Early Early Childhood Songs, Ella Jenkins. Folkways 7630.

Famous American Railroad Songs, RCA CAS 1056.

Fiedler's Favorites for Children. RCA VCS 7080.

Folk Songs for Young Folk—Animals, Vol. 1, Folkways 7677. Vol. 2,
Folkways 7642.

Hap Palmer Records. Educational Activities, Inc.
Learning Basic Skills Through Music. Vol. 1—AR 514, Vol. II—
AR 522.
Learning Basic Skills Through Music. Health and Safety. Vol. III—
AR 526.
Mod Marches, AR 527. *The Feel of Music,* AR 556.
Holiday Songs and Rhythms. AR 538.
Creative Movement and Rhythmic Exploration. AR 533.
Modern Tunes for Rhythms and Instruments. AR 532.

I Love a Marching Band. Golden Record GLP 28.

Jambo and Other Call and Response Songs, Ella Jenkins. Folkways 7661.

Jumpnastics. Educational Activities, Inc. LP 6000.
Records and teacher's manual. Requires no equipment. Perceptual-
motor activities.

Major Classics for Minors. CAS 1016e.

More Music Time and Stories, Charity Bailey. Folkways 7528.

Music, Movement, Art. Kimbo Records 7030.

Music for Movement Exploration. Educational Activities, Inc., 5090.
Children are free to create to popular music.

Music for 1's and 2's. CMS Records 649.

Music Time, Charity Bailey. Folkways 7307.

1,2,3, and Zing, Zing, Zing. Folkways 7003.
Game songs from New York City street life.

Patriotic and Morning Time Songs, Hap Palmer. Educational Activities, Inc. AR 519.

Peter, Paul, and Mommy, Peter, Paul, and Mary. Warner Bros. WS 1785. "Going to the Zoo," "Marvelous Toy," "Puff," etc.

Play Party Games. Bowmar 209, Album 1. Bowmar 210, Album 2.

Play Your Instruments and Make A Pretty Sound, Ella Jenkins. Folkways 7665.

Rhythm and Game Songs for Little Ones, Ella Jenkins. Folkways 7680.

Rhythms of Childhood, Ella Jenkins. Folkways 7653.

Seasons for Singing, Ella Jenkins. Folkways 7656.

Sensorimotor Training in the Classroom (K–3). Educational Activities Inc. AR 532.

Skip Rope, Pete Seeger. Folkways 7649.

Songs About Me Series. Kimbo Records in 4 volumes.

Songs from Sesame Street. RCA CAS 1127.

Sounds of Animals, Folkways 6124. *Sounds of My City,* Folkways 7341.

The Point. RCA LSPx 1003.

Through Children's Eyes. RCA LSP 2512.

To Move Is to Be. Educational Activities, Inc. 8060.

Train to the Zoo. Young Peoples Records.

You'll Sing a Song and I'll Sing a Song, Ella Jenkins. Folkways 7664.

BASIC SERIES PUBLICATIONS

Birchard Music Series. Evanston, Ill.: Summy-Birchard Company, 1962.

Discovering Music Together. Chicago, Ill.: Follett Pub., Co., 1970.

Exploring Music. New York: Holt, Rinehart and Winston, Inc., 2nd ed., 1971.

Growing with Music. Englewood Cliffs, N.J.: Prentice-Hall, Inc., 1963.

New Dimensions in Music. New York: American Book Company, 1974.

Rhythms to Reading. Glendale, California: Bowmar Publishing Co., 1972.

Spectrum of Music. New York: Macmillan Co., 1974.

The Magic of Music. Boston, Mass.: Ginn and Co., 1965.

This Is Music. Boston, Mass.: Allyn and Bacon, Inc., 1962.